Goat

Chinese

Horoscope

2023

By

IChingHun FengShuisu

Table of Contents

Introduce

The character of people born in the year of the GOAT

People born in this year enjoy romance, fantasies, fantasies, and art, are constantly in need of love and protection, are afraid of failure, and prefer to look at the world first. People born in this year are extremely lazy. So you prefer to associate with wealthy people, dislike people of lower social standing, and prefer convenience. Because people born in this year do not dare to make a decisive decision and do not dare to do anything unless they are confident, they must carefully consider what they will do before doing it. This year's births are unregulated. Not suitable for business, craftsman, artist, or writer, or a career that requires creativity and artistic abilities. This year's babies are romantic. Everyone is drawn to the charm because it is sensitive, gentle, and affectionate.

Strength:

When you are given the last assignment, you will do your absolute best.

Weaknesses:

You tend to regret it aloud, no matter how minor.

Love:

People born in this year are frequently successful in love and outstanding at work. And finance and love are especially fond of fantasies about love go far in particular, love someone who likes someone who is always passionate about it. When you care deeply about someone, you will give your all. You are completely disappointed when you are disappointed. People born this year, on the other hand, are not afraid of love so easily that they can be duped repeatedly. It takes a long time for people born in this year to find their soul mate, and once they do, their love life is often long.

Suitable Career:

Jobs that help people are ideal for those born in the Year of the Goat. They can be social services such as doctors, nurses, restaurants, hotels, handicrafts, arts and crafts, agriculture, or the sale of construction equipment. Construction contractors, engineers, designers, real estate workers, real estate agents, public relations officers, company employees, clerks, secretaries, lawyers, artists, singers, and actors, among other occupations, are all suitable for those born in the Year the Goat.

Year of the GOAT (Water) | (1943) & (2003)

"The Goat is not in the herd." is a person born in the year of the GOAT at the age of 80 years (1943) and 20 years (2003)

Overview

Even though the planet that orbits your destiny house this year is "Eka Star" for the senior destiny around the age of 80 years, you will receive auspicious power to visit your home. This year, you will have the opportunity to plan auspicious events in your family. It could be to welcome new members and allow them to buy expensive property into the house, move to work in a new home or earn merit for a new house. Both will have the opportunity to earn a lot of money. However, because a bad star is orbiting to focus on your destiny house this year, it is also affecting it. Trade insecurity and health issues are serious issues that must not be overlooked. This star's influence will make you easily irritated, so you must take care of your health this year.

Because the planet orbiting the destiny house this year is "Dao Tam Yak," a lucky star, for the young destiny around the age of 20. will give you what you want As a result, the research will continue this year. As a result, I ask that you work tirelessly to develop yourself to be in sync with and keep up with the situation. There will be numerous open opportunities. Both should make time to study and participate in activities. They should also be aware of car accidents, including those that occur while driving.

Career and Business

This year's work and commerce fell into a prosperous and prosperous seat for this year's senior destiny. You have the opportunity to broaden your work by investing in new ventures. At the same time, this year is ideal for finding an heir or a trusted person to take over the job and help manage the expanding workload. In terms of the young destiny, this year is yet another year in which you must constantly strive for self-improvement to be in sync with and keep up with the situation. There will be numerous open opportunities. It will increase your knowledge and experience. by the month that has the opportunity to wait for the destiny in both age cycles, namely the 2nd month of China (6 Mar. - 4 Apr.), the 5th month of China (6 Jun. - 6 Jul.), the 6th month of China(7 Jul. – 7 Aug.) and the 10th month of China (7 Nov. – 6 Dec.), but if entering the following months, including the 12th month of China (5 Jan. – 3 Feb.) 1st month of China (4 Feb. – 5 Mar.), 9th month of China (8 Oct. – 6 Nov.), and 11th month of China (7 Dec. 22 – 5 Jan. 23) Be wary of quarrels, avoid interfering in other people's affairs, and avoid being duped, which can result in losses.

Financial

This year's two destinies' financial fortunes have fallen into a prosperous seat. According to your investment, income will flow in a variety of ways. It appears that this includes money from fortune. This year, however, the fates of both ages should be wary of well-wishers who persuade them to invest in specific businesses, request loans, or sign financial guarantees. These are all potential sources of capital loss and damage. Especially in the months when the financial turnover is down and if possible you should avoid trusting others' word of mouth: 12th month of China (5 Jan. - 3 Feb.), 1st month of China (4 Feb. - 5 Mar.), 9th month China (8 Oct. - 6 Nov.) and 11th month of China (7 Dec. 22 - 5 Jan. 23) that you should exercise extreme caution. Do not, under any circumstances, gamble or speculate on the stock lottery. Investing in illegal and immoral enterprises is strictly forbidden. In terms of the months in which the finances of the two life cycles begin to prosper, such as the 2nd month of China (6 Mar. - 4 Apr.), the 5th month of China (6 Jun. - 6 Jul.), 6th month of China (7 Jul. – 7 Aug.) and 10th month of China (7 Nov. – 6 Dec.)

Family

This year's destiny for your family is peaceful, as auspicious stars shine in their favor. Both age cycles in the house of destiny have criteria for auspicious events to occur, whether new members are added. News of the people in the house's success or marriage, as well as the opportunity to buy expensive assets into the house However, you should be aware of any unforeseen or negligent incidents that cause injury to members of the household throughout the year. Especially during the months that should be extra careful, such as the 12th month of China (5 Jan. - 3 Feb.), the 1st month of China (4 Feb. - 5 Mar.), the 9th month of China (8 Oct. – 6 Nov.) and the 11th month of China (7 Dec. 22 – 5 Jan. 23) that destiny should pay more attention to the people in the house. The use of metal tools necessitates extreme caution. Be wary of wasting money on medical treatment.

Love

This year's destiny for young love is not going to be easy; there will be arguments, and some of them will be violent. You should remain calm, avoid being emotional, and even if you are angry or resentful, keep it in mind and talk to each other rationally. If you have a problem with the ruling servants, you should consult or inform your spouse. Otherwise, some cases will be accused of secret things, which will lead to squabbles. By the month the love of the destiny of the two cycles of age quite feuds. It is easy to argue: the 12th month of China (5 Jan. – 3 Feb.), the 1st month of China (4 Feb. – 5 Mar.), the 9th month of China (8 Oct. – 6 Nov.), and the 11th month of China (7 Dec. 22 – 5 Jan. 23) that you should avoid clashes and make the girl longer. Neither intervene nor interfere with the families of others. Avoid going to places of entertainment.

Health

This year's health horoscopes for the two destinies, especially Senior, were not promising. There is always something to think about and worry about that makes me feel like I don't sleep well. I should be careful that lack of sleep causes the body to accumulate exhaustion, resulting in disease. They must also be cautious of frostbite, which is expected to spread and manifest symptoms this year. Also, be cautious of accidental slipping and falling, which can result in leg or foot injuries. Young people must be cautious about accidents to avoid being injured by hard or sharp objects traveling near and far. Especially during the month in which the destiny of both ages must add special attention, including the 12th month of China (5 Jan. – 3 Feb.), the 1st month of China (4 Feb. – 5 Mar.)., the 9th month of China (8 Oct. – 6 Nov.), and the 11th month of China (7 Dec. 22 – 5 Jan. 23). Furthermore, during this time, you should be cautious of accidents caused by both driving and traveling to foreign countries.

Year of the GOAT (Wood) | (1955) & (2015)
" The GOAT in a herd" is a person born in the year of the GOAT at the age of 68 years (1955) and 8 years (2015)

Overview
Because in this year's life cycle, the planet that orbits into your destiny house is "Jade Star," and there are also auspicious stars "Suk Luck" and "Gekxian Star" orbiting to gather and shine

brightly. This year is thus considered auspicious for the 68-year-destiny, old's as all good things will come to make his career and trade business prosper. Investments in raw materials, chemicals, precursors, and commodities, in particular, will yield favorable returns. However, for those who enjoy gambling and speculation. It won't stop you if you're just doing it for fun. But, if you want to get rich this way, I would caution you not to expect too much. This is because your income this year is entirely from your right career, rather than your fortune. There is also something you should not overlook, and that is health issues. Gastritis, intestinal disease, tracheal disease, and esophageal disease, in particular, should be monitored and controlled. Consume only clean food. Do not undervalue these things if you want to be wealthy and healthy.

Career and Business

This year, the work horoscope will be by your side, whether you pick up a project or not. Any project that is undertaken will have a bright and prosperous future. Both of the businesses for which you are responsible are doing well. As a result, this year, you should look for heirs to carry on the big event or allow your children or trusted people to come to train to support business growth. But if entering the following months, problems and obstacles will arise, namely, the 12th month of China (5 Jan. – 3 Feb.), the 1st month of China (4 Feb. – 5 Mar.), 9th month of China. (8 Oct. – 6 Nov.) and 11th month of China (7 Dec. 22 – 5 Jan. 23). Signing work contract documents must be done with caution. Be wary of people who flatter you and do not believe them. Investing in businesses that lack knowledge, including personnel management, should be done with caution. As for the months in which destiny's trade will find good progress, these are the 2nd month of China (6 Mar. - 4th Apr.) 6th month of China (7 Jul. – 7 Aug.), and the 10th month of China (7 Nov. – 6 Dec.)

The overall return will be usable for entering into a joint venture, starting a new job, and making various investments this year. But you should avoid the Chinese 1st month of China (4 Feb. – 5 Mar.), the 9th month of China (8 Oct. –

6 Nov.), and the 11th month of China (7 Dec. 22 -). 5 Jan. 23) Beware of being deceived into investing and causing damage.

Financial

Despite the high income, the fortune of this year's fortunes, there are expenses in long lines. As a result, you should prepare to manage your finances effectively. This year, the month when the financial star is falling and you should carefully manage your income and expenses, namely: 12th month of China (5 Jan. - 3 Feb.), 1st month of China (4 Feb. - 5 Mar.), 9th month of China (8 Oct. – 6 Nov.) and 11th month of China (7 Dec. 22 – 5 Jan. 23) gambling and gambling are prohibited Do not invest in any business that is illegal, immoral, or violates the law. Borrowing money and providing financial guarantees are strictly forbidden.

For the months that your finances are flowing smoothly, such as the 2nd month of China (6 Mar. – 4 Apr.), the 5th month of China (6 Jun. – 6 Jul.), the 6th month of China (7 Jul. – 7 Aug.) and the 10th month of China (7 Nov. – 6 Dec.).

Family

Your family's first half of the year will be turbulent. The stars of Hokchae bestowed auspicious power on the house of destiny in the second half of the year. (Dao Sukwasana) shines, making many events in the house run smoothly and with less tension. Both members of the household will have the opportunity to achieve fame and wealth, as well as good reconciliation. But be cautious because a killer star is also targeting the family base. As a result, be cautious of accidents and unexpected disasters. Especially the threat from burglars or robbers will create trouble. The destiny must be very careful during the following months: 12th month of China (5 Jan. - 3 Feb.), 1st month of China (4 Feb. - 5 Mar.), 9th month of China (8 Oct. – 6 Nov), and 11th month of China (7 Dec. 22 – 5 Jan. 23). During these times, you should be concerned about the health and safety of your family members. When leaving the house, valuables should not be visible. Also, make sure to keep valuables in a secure location.

Love

This year's love is easy to quarrel about. Part of this will be due to destiny's rage and inconsistency. As a result, be mindful of your own words and actions that may have an impact on the other person's feelings. In addition to having to look after him and us, being overly concerned about others will lead to the problem. And this year, I wish you to be firm rather than indifferent. Other people's words can be heard. But don't take it too seriously; you might have to divide it in half. By the end of the month, your relationship will be strained. and easily arguing: 12th month of China (5 Jan. – 3 Feb.), 1st month of China (4 Feb. – 5 Mar.), 9th month of China (8 Oct. – 6 Nov.), and the 11th month of China (7 Dec. 22 – 5 Jan. 23). Do not meddle in other people's families, and avoid going to entertainment venues because they could be infected with the disease and cause a slew of issues.

Health

This year's health, even in the middle However, if you become ill, you will be able to locate a doctor who specializes in good medicine.

However, it is still possible that the disease will interfere with the rest of the year. As a result, they must exercise greater caution and adhere to stricter food hygiene standards. Grilling, grilling, and barbecue foods should be avoided. It will also cause overheating of the body and symptoms to appear this year. You should also be cautious of high blood pressure and heart disease. For the months in which you need to take special care of your health, these are the 12th month of China (5 Jan. – 3 Feb.), 1st month of China (4 Feb. – 5 Mar.), 9th month of China (8 Oct. - 6 Nov.) and the 11th month of China (7 Dec. 22 - 5 Jan. 23). If you experience any unusual symptoms, you should consult a doctor. Because treatment from the start has a better chance of success.

Year of the GOAT (Fire) | (1967)

" The Goat in the Grass " is a person born in the year of the GOAT at the age of 56 years (1967)

Overview

Because the planet orbiting your destiny this year is "Eka Star," even though entering this year is considered a good year for destiny. The work will have a distinct outcome. There is always the possibility of expanding a business. There will be good news in the family about family members' academic or professional success. Both of you will have the opportunity to move house, move shop, or open a new shop if you meet the criteria for purchasing an expensive property. However, due to the influence of "Eka Star," the mood of this year's destiny frequently fluctuates, irritable, impulsive, impulsive, and acts as you wish. Because there is a villainous star "Kuo Hu" (lawsuit star) in your destiny this year to kill and harass them together. As a result, they should be wary of disputes such as lawsuits or issues with government agencies. For example, taxes on licenses or trade investments that may be illegal, such as copyright, plagiarism, or product falsification. Be cautious; being punished by criminals will be disastrous. Especially during the 12th month of China (5 Jan. – 3 Feb.), the 1st month of China (4 Feb. – 5 Mar.), the 9th month of China (8 Oct. – 6 Nov.) and the 11th month of China (7 Dec 22 – 5 Jan 23), however, during the year, an auspicious star known as "Sam Tai" will shine into the house of fate to assist. Trade and sales investment will be bright and smooth. There will be new channels or products that will provide you with adequate returns.

Career and Business

The fortunes of this year's work are very good. Those who work this year will see the success of their efforts. Those who trade will see a bright trading direction and a tendency to expand or branch out. Those who invest in raw materials, chemicals, commodities, and start-ups will benefit the most. However, because "Dao Lawsuit" is aimed at the corner in destiny, the various trades that you are responsible for this year cannot ignore the law. Both must be more careful not to be harassed by enemies or competitors, and to be aware that there will be interpersonal conflicts in the chaotic organization that will not end. Especially during the months that do not support you and will encounter obstacles, problems include: the 12th month of China (5 Jan. - 3 Feb.), 1st month of China (4 Feb. - 5 Mar.), 9th month of China (8 Oct. - 6 Nov.) and 11th month of China (7 Dec. 22 - 5 Jan. 23)

As for the months in which his trade is bright and prosperous, such as the 2nd month of China (6 Mar. - 4 April), the 5th month of China (6 Jun. - 6 Jul.), the 6th month of China (7 Jul. – 7 Aug.) and the 10th month of China (7 Nov. – 6 Dec.).

Financial

Around this age, the fortune of fortune and money of the Year of the Goat is not stable. You must be sick of adjusting your liquidity and trying to find enough income to cover your expenses. Even at the beginning and end of the year, there will be plenty of cash inflows, both direct income, and windfall. However, you should not be greedy and greedy, and you should be content with your wealth earned in good faith. Especially if entering the following month, your finances will stumble, including the 12th month of China (5 Jan. – 3 Feb.), 1st month of China (4 Feb. – 5 Mar.), 9th month of China (8 Oct. – 6 Nov) and 11th month of China (7 Dec. 22 – 5 Jan. 23). You should not lend money to anyone or sign financial guarantees to help anyone, and you should not invest. Engaging in illegal or immoral activity. Take care not to avoid the penalties. Criminals must be punished. As for the months in which your finances have good liquidity, they are 2nd month of China (6 Mar. – 4 Apr.), 5th month of China (6 Jun. – 6 Jul.), 6th month of China (7 Jul. – 7 Aug.) and the 10th month of China (7 Nov. – 6 Dec.).

Family

The Chao Destiny family as a whole was considered peaceful. Even if there appear to be some conflicts, there are some problems, but dealing with them is within your grasp. But when entering the 12th month of China (5 Jan. – 3 Feb.), the 1st month of China (4 Feb. – 5 Mar.), 9th month of China (8 Oct. – 6 May). Yor.)

and the 11th month of China (7 Dec. 22 – 5 Jan. 23) should be cautious about lost or stolen valuables, as well as causing minors harm.

This year, relatives and friends will ask you how to choose a relationship, which should be well thought out. Be wary of people who come hoping for hidden benefits that will cause you trouble and property loss. You should be especially careful during the 1st month of China (4 Feb. – 5 Mar.), the 9th month of China (8 Oct. – 6 Nov.) and the 11th month of China (7 Dec. 22 – 5 Jan. 23) Furthermore, please avoid getting involved in a friendly conflict. Problems in lawsuits or illegal activities, in particular, because they may be dragged to suffer as well.

Love

Your love horoscope for this year necessitates a great deal of patience, so please be patient with any dissatisfaction or dissatisfaction that arises in the relationship. There must be an examination of the flaws. And there are gains on both sides. Do not be arrogant, and exercise caution before making any decisions. Consider family and children first. So avoid getting emotional, especially when your rage is directed at the other person. However, it will only allow you to talk without knowing anything. Especially if it enters the month where love and relationships are fragile and easy to break, such as the 12th month of China (5 Jan. – 3 Feb.), the 1st month of China (4 Feb. – 5 Mar.), the 9th month of China (8 Oct. – 6 Nov.) and the 11th month of China (7 Dec. 22 – 5 Jan. 23). Please avoid getting involved in other people's family matters. Take the time to listen and choose words that are considerate of the other person's feelings. Don't just go outside in a cold and indifferent mood in search of something pleasant. Be aware that visiting entertainment venues can result in illnesses, as well as loss of property and reputation.

Health

This year, the fate is in good health, which will lead to more commercial work. However, the workload is full of faces, resulting in a lack of neglect of eating and living, which may lead to disease due to health neglect. Especially during the following months that you should increase your health consciousness especially: the 12th month of China (5 Jan. - 3 Feb.), China (4 Feb. - 5 Mar.), the 9th month of China (8 Oct. – 6 Nov.), and the 11th month of China (7 Dec. 22 – 5 Jan. 23). Furthermore, you must be more cautious about accidents both at work and on the road. Driving in vehicles that are subject to alcohol checkpoints should be avoided. If it exceeds the standard, it will not only be fined but may also be criminally prosecuted due to the lawsuit star aiming at an angle. There is a greater opportunity to gain experience in legal and litigation matters. As a result, you should exercise greater caution.

Year of the GOAT (Earth) | (1979)
" The Goat in distress" is a person born in the year of the GOAT at the age of 44 years (1979)

Overview
Because the planet that orbits your destiny this year is "Kok Ying Star" (Jade Star), this is the year that the Year of the Goat around this age has a good chance for one year. The trade business and job duties will go smoothly, and the job's direction is bright. And trade tends to

expand due to the auspicious stars' influence on delivery. However, you should continue to strive; everything still depends on your ability to break through. Even if your fortunes improve this year and you find auspicious power to help you. However, you must be wary of the evil star "Tho Huai," who takes over and disrupts your destiny. which will cause your mind to tremble, as well as a lack of concentration Only interested in the taste of affection. Both will result in genuine love, cracks, and arguments, leaving the family unhappy. However, it is believed that he is still fortunatc bccause the auspicious stars "Koiing" and "Sam Tai" (God Satai) shine to assist him. on the road to enchantment As a result, being conscious and capable of returning to the truth in life is sufficient.

Career and Business

This year, the power of progress has returned to the fated house, so it is an excellent opportunity for you to demonstrate your wisdom and workability to those around you. To increase the workload and improve the quality of the work. for sales or store expansion to increase investment. Alternatively, stepping up to become a business owner will result in cooperation from those around you. However, this would be contingent on diligence and perseverance. Don't let the stimuli distract you from achieving your goals. Especially the months in which his work is prosperous, such as the 2nd month of China (6 Mar. – 4 Apr.), the 5th month of China (6 Jun. – 6 Jul.), the 6th month of China (7 Jul. - 7 Aug.) and China (7 Nov. - 6 Dec.) However, you need to be careful of the months when your work will be very congested with obstacles. 12th month of China (5 Feb – 3 Feb.),1st month of China (4 Feb. – 5 Mar.),9th month of China (8 Oct. – 6 Nov.), and 11th month of China (7 Dec. 22 – 5 Jan.23).

Financial

Your ability and dedication to focus on one of your major matters will determine your financial fortunes this year. Being extremely diligent will result in a great deal. As a result, you should focus your efforts on your responsibilities. You should plan to take good care of your finances in the coming month. Because there is a possibility of stumbling, such as the 12th month of China (5 Jan. – 3 Feb.), the 1st month of China (4 Feb. – 5 Mar.), 9th month of China (8 Oct. – 6th). Nov.) and the 11th month of China (7 Dec. 22 – 5 Jan. 23). You should refrain from lending money to others. and should not invest in companies that violate the law Whether it's tax evasion or copyright infringement, it can lead to lawsuits and property loss.

As for the month in which your financial fortunes return to flow smoothly, there is liquidity: 2nd month of China (6 Mar. – 4 Apr.), 5th month of China (6 Jun. – 6 Jul.), 6th month of China (7 Jul. – 7 Aug.) and 10th month of China (7 Nov. – 6 Dec.).

Family

This year's events in the destiny family are fortunate, especially in the safety of the home because there is a criterion that items will fall from a height to cause harm, including equipment or furniture that is fixed to some parts may be damaged, posing a risk to people in the house. Furthermore, be wary of fire and heat accidents, as well as electrical wiring and gas stoves, and be wary of people in the house who are careless with fire. Fire or explosion negligence can lead to injury and tragedy. The month that you have to be especially careful of unexpected events during the 12th month of China (5 Jan. – 3 Feb.), the 1st month of China (4 Feb. – 5 Mar.), the 9th month of China (8 Oct. – 6 Nov.) and the 11th month of China (7 Dec. 22 – 5 Jan. 23). In addition, beware of lost or stolen valuables.

Love

Due to the peach blossom devil star "Tho Huai" orbiting to harass and harass, this year's destiny is on the love side. This is a good story for someone who is still single by destiny. Because you will be attracted to a large number of people of the opposite sex and will have the opportunity to study and build relationships. Those who have a lover or partner, on the other hand, will have the opportunity to divert their attention. Acting like a fool can easily lead to breakups and arguments, so please learn to control yourself. Don't let the brief intimacy become too much of an issue. Especially during the months when love is fragile, it is easy to argue, such as the 12th month of China (5 Jan. - 3 Feb.), and the 1st month of China (4 Feb. - 5 Mar.). The 9th month of China (8 Oct. - 6 Nov.) and the 11th month of China (7 Dec. 22 - 5 Jan. 23).

Health

Your overall health is good this year. You should devote your strength to your work. You can produce a large amount of work and work. Money will come in. Don't get drunk with a group of travel-loving friends. You wander around and rummage for entertainment venues. Because sleep deprivation and insufficient rest can lead to the development of diseases. By the month you need to be careful of health problems that will come up, namely: 12th month of China (5 Jan. - 3 Feb.), 1st month of China (4 Feb. - 5th Mar.), 9th month of China (8 Oct – 6 Nov.) and the 11th month of China (7 Dec 22 – 5 Jan 23). Furthermore, caution should be exercised during work and travel accidents. And be cautious when driving a car on the road.

Year of the GOAT (Gold) | (1991)

" The Goat is extremely powerful" is a person born in the year of the GOAT at the age of 32 years (1991)

Overview

Because the planet orbiting your destiny house this year is the villain "Eka," who will influence you, is frequently irritable and irritable, prefers to be introverted, and dislikes dealing with people. You will need to be extra diligent and patient this year to get through it. Avoid hanging out with friends who enjoy dressing up as gangsters. You could be hit by crossfire, and you could be in danger. During the 12th month of China (5 Jan. – 3 Feb.), the 1st month of China (4 Feb. – 5 Mar.), the 9th month of China (8 Oct. – 6 Nov.), and the 11th month of China (7 Dec 22 – 5 Jan 23) there will be people to come and find Please be patient and escape first for safety.

Career and Business

In terms of work, avoid using emotions in both work and relationships this year. They must always maintain and strengthen positive relationships with their coworkers. Those pursuing a master's or doctorate must be mindful of being distracted by stimuli and other provocations in their surroundings. Another thing to keep in mind this year is that if you go with a group of friends who like to cause trouble, you will end up in trouble with the number tail. Especially during the months that you should be very careful, such as the 12th month of China (5 Jan. – 3 Feb.), the 1st month of China (4 Feb. – 5 Mar.), the 9th month of China (8 Oct. Dec. - 6 Nov.) and the 11th month of China (7 Dec. 22 - 5 Jan. 23). Working or engaging in various activities I ask that you be extra cautious during this time. because there are criteria for being duped into being responsible for a crime he did not commit or because he may be injured as a result of a crossfire.

During the month when work and investment are bright and prosperous, such as the 2nd month of China (6 Mar. - 4 Apr.), the 5th month of China (6 Jun. - 6 Jul.), the 6th month of China

(7 Jul. – 7 Aug.) and the 10th month of China (7 Nov. – 6 Dec.).

Financial

This year, your financial fortune will be ordinary income. However, be wary of the disastrous consequences of intoxication and the greed of wanting to get back from the speculative gambling that will make you sick and deplete your liquidity. In particular, you should avoid speculative investments during the following months: the 12th month of China (Jan. 5 - Feb. 3), the 1st month of China (4 Feb. - 5 Mar.), the 9th month of China (8 Oct - 6 Nov.) and the 11th month of China (7 Dec 22 - 5 Jan. 24) Borrowing money and signing guarantees on behalf of others are both prohibited. Be wary of unexpected expenses that will deplete your funds and cause your wallet to shrink. For the months that your finances are in good shape, i.e. 2nd month of China (6 Mar. – 4 Apr.), the 5th month of China (6 Jun. – 6 Jul.), 6th month of China (7 Jul. – 7 Aug.) and the 10th month of China (7 Nov. – 6 Dec.).

Family

For this year, the first six months of the year will be tumultuous, with disagreements between members of the household. or unforeseen health problems or bleeding accidents that will occur among household members. Especially during the following months in which the family will experience turmoil, namely: 12th month of China (5 Jan. - 3 Feb.), 1st month of China (4 Feb. - 5 Mar), 9th month of China (8 Oct. – 6 Nov) and 11th month of China (7 Dec. 66 – 5 Jan. 67). You should be cautious about home security during this time. and look after the people in the house so that they can reconcile without arguing

The horoscopes for this year are not favorable. Be wary of ill-willed friends who drag them into taking responsibility for the lawsuit even though you are unaware of it. Especially during the 1st month of China (4 Feb. – 5 Mar.), the 9th month of China (8 Oct. – 6 Nov.), and the 11th month of China (7 Dec. 22 – 5 Jan. 23) You should avoid friends who frequently invite you to travel. Don't get involved in a disagreement between friends. Be wary of becoming involved in a legal dispute.

Love

This year, there will be an opportunity to meet the opposite sex which is interesting and should investigate the possibility of living together rather than the so-called friend. However, love usually begins with a friend and progresses to the next level. However, you should be careful during the 12th month of China (5 Jan. – 3 Feb.), the 1st month of China (4 Feb. – 5 Mar.), the 9th month of China (8 Oct. – 6 Nov.) and the 11th month of China (7 Dec. 22 – 5 Jan. 23) should exercise caution when using words that are not intended to cause misunderstandings. Ask yourself if you are ready to be serious or if you want to start a relationship first. Because if you are unsure, don't just give the other party hope. Furthermore, do not interfere with the love relationships of other couples.

Health

This year's physical health is moderate, but you should always take care of yourself and take care of yourself. Try to get enough sleep at night. Choose clean and sanitary food. Hot foods should be avoided. Beware of self-torture from indulgences. Furthermore, something you should be more cautious of is the crossfire from an accident. It is still dangerous to travel and drive. Be on the lookout for any unexpected dangers that may arise. Especially during the months that do not support you, such as the 12th month of China (5 Jan. – 3 Feb.), the 1st month of China (4 Feb. – 5 Mar.), the 9th month of China (8 Oct. - 6 Nov.) and 11th month of China (7 Dec. 22 - 5 Jan. 23).

Chinese Astrology Horoscope for Each Month

Month 12 in the Tiger Year (6 Jan 23 - 3 Feb 23)

Begin the new year with a clash between your zodiac sign and your destiny. As a result, the house of the zodiac was demolished and collapsed. There are numerous obstacles to trade work during this period. Seek assistance from an adult. You will be guided so that the product can be drained quickly and some issues can be resolved so that you can move on. Important things to do during this period Please be patient when engaging in high-investment, high-responsibility activities. You should seek advice from an adult before making a decision, and you should maintain contact with both old and new friends while remaining calm. Be respectful, don't brag, and don't get too caught up in your thoughts because you may have to be alone in the end.

This income is low in terms of salary, and the expenditure is excessive. During this time, liquidity will be constrained, causing problems. As a result, you should stick to sufficiency measures, use as much as possible, and avoid speculative outside investments. Never lend money to others. Don't make any promises. Avoid gambling and gambling-related activities, including illegal business.

During this time, members of the family must ensure the safety of those in the house and be on the lookout for unexpected incidents that may result in injuries to family members.

On the subject of health, be mindful of drinking and eating hygiene, and avoid being careless while traveling to avoid becoming ill from hidden diseases.

On the plus side, love is easy and relationships flourish, but the outlook for investments in various fields remains bleak.

Support Days: 1 Jan., 5 Jan., 9 Jan., 13 Jan., 17 Jan., 21 Jan., 25 Jan., 29 Jan.
Lucky Days: 12 Jan., 24 Jan.
Misfortune Days: 7 Jan., 19 Jan., 31 Jan
Bad Days: 4 Jan., 6 Jan., 16 Jan., 28 Jan., 30 Jan.

Month 1 in the Rabbit Year (4 Feb 23 - 5 Mar 23)
This month, your fortunes are like a graph that is falling in work and business. There will be significant unevenness issues. Those born in the Year of the Goat should be cautious and plan ahead of time for protection. Accelerate the detection of bugs and their resolution of them. Don't wait until it's too late.

You must be cautious of people who dislike your face during this time of work. Conflicts from financial and accounting audits should be avoided. This month, you should focus on developing positive relationships with those around you. Prepare your work and financial factors, and remind yourself that when it comes to investments, don't just look at the pretty numbers. Regardless of long-term interests, the only show in front.

This month, your fortunes are like a graph that is falling in work and business. There will be significant unevenness issues. Those born in the Year of the Goat should be cautious and plan ahead of time for protection. Accelerate the detection of bugs and their resolution of them. Don't wait until it's too late.

You must be cautious of people who dislike your face during this time of work. Conflicts from financial and accounting audits should be avoided. This month, you should focus on developing positive relationships with those around you. Prepare your work and financial factors, and remind yourself that when it comes to investments, don't just look at the pretty numbers. Regardless of long-term interests, the only show in front.

Fate is not in good health these days. Please be cautious of high blood pressure. A hidden disease that will manifest symptoms Take precautions to avoid food poisoning. In addition, the risk of injury from travel accidents necessitates caution.

Support Days: 2 Feb., 6 Feb., 10 Feb., 14 Feb., 18 Feb., 22 Feb., 26 Feb.
Lucky Days: 5 Feb., 17 Feb.
Misfortune Days: 12 Feb., 24 Feb.

Bad Days: 9 Feb., 11 Feb., 21 Feb., 23 Feb.

Month 2 in the Rabbit Year (6 Mar 23 - 5 Apr 23)

This month, many auspicious stars shine in the house of fate, assisting in smoothing trade, finding a path forward, and removing obstacles. You will discover new opportunities or channels that will help your business thrive.

This month, you should put your talents and abilities to good use and demonstrate them to others. Aside from work that appears to be admired by supervisors or adults, it also helps to spread your reputation. However, you should carefully plan your work schedule. Otherwise, minor issues will compound and become major issues later.

This salary horoscope landed in a wealthy seat. There will be numerous cash inflows. Neither trading, selling as a broker, nor successfully negotiating a trade business. There will also be more floating fortunes coming through.

During this time, you will experience auspicious events and receive good news from your family. A new addition, the success of the people in the house, the purchase of more expensive assets, or the purchase of a new home are all possibilities.

On the sweet side of love, The past feuds will be better. They will also receive assistance from relatives and friends.

Good health, and full of energy, but you should be careful of accidents while using the car on the road. Especially after a party, if alcohol gets into your mouth, you shouldn't sit in front of the steering wheel because you might get into an accident.

Support Days: 2 Mar, 6 Mar., 10 Mar., 14 Mar., 18 Mar., 22 Mar., 26 Mar., 30 Mar.
Lucky Days: 1 Mar, 13 Mar., 25 Mar.
Misfortune Days: 8 Mar, 20 Mar.
Bad Days: 5 Mar, 7 Mar., 17 Mar., 19 Mar., 29 Mar., 31 Mar.

Month 3 in the Rabbit Year (6 Apr 23 - 5 May 23)
This month, the Destiny of the Year of the Goat's life path has taken a downward turn. Many impediments and inconsistencies have arisen. Work problems, in particular, are swarming in, causing you to be stressed. Please keep in mind, however, that problems are meant to be solved, not discouraged. You should change your way of thinking and what you expect to happen. Be wary of colleagues, competitors, or employees demanding fairness during this period of destiny work. The corrective action must be based on a middle path of fairness and compromise.

What you should do this month is when a lot of things come at you at once. You must exert control over yourself to remain calm and resolve the most critical issues first. Don't be apathetic. Otherwise, a minor issue could grow into a major issue that is difficult to resolve.

This salary horoscope ran into a wrangle. There will be a leak point, resulting in the loss of capital liquidity. Investments must be made with caution, as they may be deceived. You should not invest in or be greedy for things you do not deserve.

During this time, no one in the family should be careless about unexpected accidents. Take care not to injure anyone in the house with metal objects.

Love is neither good nor bad. Just don't add any more fuel; it'll last long enough.

In terms of health, keep an eye out for liver disease, intestinal disease, food poisoning, and various infectious diseases.

This month's joint stock or investment is not appropriate and should be postponed.

Support Days: 3 Apr., 7 Apr., 11 Apr., 15 Apr., 19 Apr., 23 Apr., 27 Apr.
Lucky Days: 6 Apr., 18 Apr., 30 Apr.
Misfortune Days: 1 Apr., 13 Apr., 25 Apr.
Bad Days: 10 Apr., 12 Apr., 22 Apr., 24 Apr.

Month 4 in the Rabbit Year (6 May 23 - 5 Jun 23)
Your destiny has dropped again this month if you were born in the Year of the Goat. Trade relations are going well. Be wary of interfering incidents during this time. Makes you have to adjust in one aspect, so you should do your best to take care of the work in your responsibilities. Do not rely on interfering with others' work. In addition to the criterion of your destiny at this time, falling into the seat hesitantly concerned about your back may cause you to miss out on a good opportunity.

During this time, you should make courageous decisions. Sometimes there isn't enough time to make a choice. Others who are more considerate will come before you to snatch and cut. Then you may have to sit and think about it later.

This salary horoscope is typical. You still have a consistent income, but your expenses have not decreased. There is little extra money from speculation and gambling with luck. So don't expect too much, and it's not worth it. Also, exercise caution if you intend to invest in dishonest trading. Beware, the punishment will catch up with you.

During this time, the family will be happy and smooth. However, especially with those close to you, you should always speak with kindness and concern for their health.

In terms of love, be wary of your flaws, which can lead to unintentional and emotional affairs, resulting in inadvertent stories.

For your good, but be wary of accidents that could result in arm or leg injury.

Starting a new job or entering into a joint venture at this time is not appropriate.

Support Days: 1 May., 5 May., 9 May., 13 May., 17 May., 21 May., 25 May., and 29 May.

Lucky Days: 12 May., and 24 May.
Misfortune Days: 7 May., 19 May., 31 May.
Bad Days: 4 May., 6 May., 16 May., 18 May., 28 May., 30 May.

Month 5 in the Rabbit Year (6 Jun 23 - 6 Jul 23)
In terms of destiny, even if you have only experienced some difficulties in the last month, there are still some accumulated issues. So you should go over the objectives you set. Even if some obstacles exist, they should be addressed one by one following the cause. Some issues that, for the time being, cannot be resolved before the end of the story. Just don't give up and become disheartened. It's because your future base is still ripe for success. It would be a shame to leave now without fighting. However, when facing serious problems until reaching a dead end, there will be a light at the end of the tunnel, someone reaching out to you.

There is frequently a story on the financial fortune for you to take money out of your pocket. As a result, we must locate the leak and repair it before it causes friction. However, this floating fortune will have the opportunity to see. However, it should not be difficult to spend in the hope of retaliation because it will cause more pain. To be safe, always keep a gold reserve on hand.

Family horoscope, members who are peaceful and reconciling.

However, the fate of love may find a seat of dissatisfaction due to either party or one party. Can't give the other party enough time, which leads to arguments. You must also be firm and restrained. Don't expose yourself to too many external stimuli.

For your health, not for a serious disease.

Your family and friends are always there for you.

However, when investing in various fields, be cautious not to fall into the trap of losing property.

Support Days: 2 Jun., 6 Jun., 10 Jun., 14 Jun., 18 Jun., 22 Jun., 26 Jun., 30 Jun.
Lucky Days: 5 Jun., 17 Jun., 29 Jun.
Misfortune Days: 12 Jun., 24 Jun.
Bad Days: 9 Jun., 11 Jun., 21 Jun., 23 Jun.

Month 6 in the Rabbit Year (7 Jul 23 - 7 Aug 23)
This month, your destiny as a Goat born in the Year of the Goat remains bright. Meeting the partner month and having auspicious stars to support it is a good opportunity to improve your health. We can't let time pass without improving our work and putting our knowledge and abilities to use. As a result, you should hurry to plan and prepare for the creation of works during this auspicious month. Make sales to increase the amount of money in your pocket; your hard work and determination will not be in vain.

This salary horoscope is considered normal; the money received from luck floats sufficiently. But don't be greedy or your fortune will vanish. Even regular income continues to flow normally. However, if you spend more then you have the right to a financial shortage.

There will be challenges for you to overcome in your commercial work during this time. Workplace conflicts, both management and personnel, should be avoided. Compromise is the best way to resolve the current conflict. It is preferable to reduce the problem than to persevere to overcome it, which benefits no one.

There is peace and harmony in your family.

As for love, it still requires support and should be given more care and attention to remain sweet.

Health horoscopes are recommended at this stage because, in addition to being cautious of accidents while at work and traveling, you should also be cautious of illness.

This month is not promising for joint ventures, new job starts, or investments in various fields. So, if you just study the guidelines and don't invest any money, you'll be fine.

Support Days: 4 Jul., 8 Jul., 12 Jul., 16 Jul., 20 Jul., 24 Jul., 28 Jul.
Lucky Days: 11 Jul., 23 Jul.
Misfortune Days: 6 Jul., 18 Jul., 30 Jul.

Bad Days: 3 Jul., 5 Jul., 15 Jul., 17 Jul., 27 Jul., 29 Jul.

Month 7 in the Rabbit Year (8 Aug 23 - 7 Sep 23)
This month, destiny has discovered a perilous line, causing the zero-life graph to fall from orbit. Work will face challenges. Businesses will face disagreements and challenges from competitors.

This month, here's what you should do. Every activity necessitates a dedication to work. Under the obstacles that must be overcome to successfully exit the enclave, one cannot be lazy to survive.

Horoscopes, this salary, discovered the monsoon, earn less, pay more, do not gamble, gamble, do not engage in illegal business because they may face criminal charges.

Work must be physically and emotionally exhausting because there will be numerous problems to deal with at the same time, ranging from insufficient funds to accounting issues.

Accounts receivable do not pay on time, and some will be written off. On the management side, there are frequent conflicts both within and outside the organization. As a result, organizational conflicts should be addressed first, followed by a search for emergency funds to supplement liquidity.

Be wary of losing your property on the side of your family. As a result, spending should be done with extreme caution and avoid interfering with gambling.

Your love is still in good condition; love each other more and make time to add more love to each other's lives.

Overall health is good, except for diseases caused by climate change, cold symptoms, and insufficient rest.

This month is not favorable for relatives or investments. It is legal to be duped and lose benefits.

Support Days: 1 Aug., 5 Aug., 9 Aug., 13 Aug., 17 Aug., 21 Aug., 25 Aug., 29 Aug.

Lucky Days: 4 Aug., 16 Aug., 28 Aug.
Misfortune Days: 11 Aug., 23 Aug.
Bad Days: 8 Aug., 10 Aug., 20 Aug., 22 Aug.

Month 8 in the Rabbit Year (8 Sep 23 - 7 Oct 23)
This month's destiny is due to moving to meet the alliance, as well as many auspicious stars shining into your destiny house. As a result, both their work and their relationships with those around them are improving.

Work and trade have found a way forward and will aid in the resolution of problems and obstacles. The project he had hoped for began to come together. This is an excellent opportunity to engage in activities that require you to take risks.

What you should do this month is seize the calm winds and rush to build a portfolio of expanding sales to make up for what you lost, particularly capital depletion.

This salary horoscope is favorable. Cash inflows will come in two forms. Salary and sales income are both fixed sources of income. Additionally, extra money from commissions or brokers. as well as winnings from gambling However, you should use it wisely. Because fortune can sometimes reveal whether you are financially stable or not.

Families uncover auspicious power. There will be auspicious opportunities to move into a new home, renovate the house, or host auspicious events in the house.

Sweet, compassionate, sympathetic lovers understand you better for this month's love. May you be firm, honest, and face-to-face because marriage is a fulfilling experience. If there is a problem, please assist in discussing and discussing. The crisis will end. But should avoid alcohol, cigarettes, and drugs for overall good health.

If you run into problems, your relatives will be able to assist you.

You can participate in this month's joint venture by investing. But don't put everything into it.

Support Days: 2 Sep, 6 Sep., 10 Sep, 14 Sep, 18 Sep., 22 Sep., 26 Sep., 30 Sep.
Lucky Days: 9 Sep, 21 Sep.
Misfortune Days: 4 Sep., 16 Sep., 28 Sep.
Bad Days: 1 Sep, 3 Sep., 13 Sep, 15 Sep, 25 Sep., 27 Sep.

Month 9 in the Rabbit Year (8 Oct 23 - 6 Nov 23)
This month, your destiny criterion has avoided the perilous streak. Many improvements have been made. Businesses and trades have resumed their original course.

This month, you should exercise caution in all of your work activities. Tell yourself to be strong, and don't let a single mistake bring your troops down.

Job luck will bring in customers, but you must dare to decide, dare to do, and dare to accept. Dare to experiment with something new. Dare to forge a new path. The project will be a success.

This salary horoscope is like being stuck in neutral. Do not pay out if there is an entry. Even if it sounds appealing, it will harm your credit and make no one want to be in a relationship with you. Because there is no new product replenishment if your product is sold out. Customers in the future will also flee.

Every step of the way during this financial period, there will be a reason to take money out of your pocket, so you must know how to spend. To maintain financial liquidity, avoid unnecessary extravagant purchases.

The family horoscopes for this month are safe and happy.

In terms of love, although it is not the same as before, it is unavoidable that the person you rejected will return. If you return with positive feelings. You should be optimistic about your future happiness.

You should always take care of yourself during this period of health. Grilled, salty, and extremely sweet foods should be avoided. All of them will result in diseases.

Be aware that there will be disagreements between relatives and friends during this time. To keep a good relationship, you should be willing to compromise on certain issues.

Joining a joint venture and making investments should be avoided when starting a new job.

Support Days: 4 Oct., 8 Oct., 12 Oct., 16 Oct., 20 Oct., 24 Oct., 28 Oct.
Lucky Days: 3 Oct., 15 Oct., 27 Oct.
Misfortune Days: 10 Oct., 22 Oct.
Bad Days: 7 Oct., 9 Oct., 19 Oct., 21 Oct., 31 Oct.

Month 10 in the Rabbit Year (7 Nov 23 - 6 Dec 23)

The road of your life suddenly lit up as destiny entered this month, the black clouds that had accumulated from the previous month had faded. Everything appeared to be fluid and agile at the time. It will be able to benefit regardless of which project, the outstanding project is picked up to dust the new dust. You will have a lot of job opportunities during this time. You should be quick to seize those good opportunities for them to flourish and prosper. Don't squander your time.

The most important thing to remember during this time is to avoid acting arrogantly because you may irritate those around you, which will not benefit you.

This salary horoscope is quite favorable; there will be money inflows from two sources: salary for sales, extra money from extra work, and money from gambling luck floating. Even if you have a lot of money, you should be cautious with your spending this month. Should save money and add income-generating channels for circulation.

Members of the peaceful family are in harmony, love, and harmony, according to the horoscope.

The love aspect is sweet and has been improving in recent months. If you are single, this month is a good time to ask for love or a marriage proposal. However, for those of you who already have a partner, love has been improving in recent months.

Your health is in good shape, but don't underestimate the importance of exercise in building muscle.

Good relatives, on the other hand, will have the opportunity to participate in public service, help society, or go out to do meritorious activities together.

This month has a promising outlook for joint ventures, new job starts, and various investments.

Support Days: 1 Nov., 5 Nov., 9 Nov., 13 Nov., 17 Nov., 21 Nov., 25 Nov., 29 Nov.
Lucky Days: 8 Nov., 20 Nov.
Misfortune Days: 3 Nov., 15 Nov., 27 Nov.
Bad Days: 2 Nov., 12 Nov., 14 Nov., 24 Nov., 26 Nov.

Month 11 in the Rabbit Year (7 Dec 23 - 5 Jan 24)
This month, Goat Destiny's life path encounters a dangerous streak, causing his destiny to fall low. Every activity that will take place must not be underestimated.

This month, here's what you should do. The wings are knowing how to dodge, and the dodge is the tail. Many of the issues that have arisen during this time are unable to be addressed. To negotiate, one must remain calm. Try not to argue.

Conflicts should be avoided in the field of trade. Please refrain from being aggressive with your colleagues, subordinates, and family members. You can caution them to provide reasons. But it wasn't as if betraying in front of others meant unknowingly becoming part of an enemy formation.

This salary's horoscopes fall on the seat and lose money. Any wish for fortune and good fortune should be avoided. Neither should they invest in new ventures. Do not lend money to others, even if you can help with guarantees.

The family must exercise extreme caution when it comes to the health of the elderly in the home. Take care not to get sick or experience any unexpected events. Furthermore, valuables should not be worn as a result of temptation. Because they may be attacked as well as robbed, and they must be wary of minors or their servants secretly stealing belongings.

There may be issues that hurt you on the side of love; stick to the principle of forgiveness and it will pass.

You frequently suffer from headaches, colds, or allergies. Also, be wary of gastritis, intestinal disease, food poisoning, and other infectious diseases.

This period cannot be trusted for entering a joint venture, starting a new job, or making various investments because there is a risk of being duped.

Support Days: 3 Dec., 7 Dec., 11 Dec., 15 Dec., 19 Dec., 23 Dec., 27 Dec, 31 Dec.
Lucky Days: 2 Dec., 14 Dec., 26 Dec.
Misfortune Days: 9 Dec., 21 Dec.
Bad Days: 6 Dec., 8 Dec., 18 Dec., 20 Dec., 30 Dec.

Amulet for The Year of the Goat
"Duowen Tianwang hold Umbrella"

This year, those born in the Year of the Goat should establish and worship sacred objects. "Duowen Tianwang holds a magical umbrella" to enhance your fortune by placing it on your desk or cash desk to ask for His Majesty's power to help protect you from danger and spread your majesty's peace. There is progress and prosperity in the business that you do, and you help to bless the business, making it smooth and fulfilling, and bringing peace and happiness to destiny.

(Note: You can see the direction in which the sacred object should be established at the end of your life cycle.)

Chapter one of the Department of Advanced Feng Shui discusses the gods who will descend and reside in the annual Mi Keng (House of Destiny). Which god can inspire both you and the blame for your fate that year? When this is the case, worshiping the gods who come down to reside in the same year of your birth is thought to be the most beneficial and affecting. To rely on the gods' prestige, he assists in protecting while his destiny is low and misfortune is reduced. At the same time, I'd like to request your blessing to help the business run as smoothly as possible. Bring you and your family luck and prosperity.

Those born in the Year of the Goat or the Mi Keng (House of Destiny) fall under the sign of BI. This year, before you even consider doing any work. Should be more cautious and cautious. Although there are auspicious stars that shine in the horoscope, this results in the direction of work-trade progress. Investment has a bright future, but because bad stars are orbiting in the fated house, it is difficult to focus. Be wary of slander and frustration this year, as they can easily lead to conflicts with others. There will also be difficulties as a result of large expenditures that exceed expectations. If you are considering engaging in any form of speculation, be wary of those who will come to deceive you. To avoid chronic disease, you should take extra care of your health. Please try to keep your emotions under control when you're in love. If you do not want the relationship to end. If you want to avoid disasters, you should make and wear amulets. "Duowen Tianwang holds the magical umbrella" to request his majesty's assistance in breaking the bad luck and granting him bright and prosperous wisdom in the development of business and trade progress. Everything you wished for will come true soon.

He is considered one of the "Sue Tian Wang" (Sue Tian Aung) or the Four Great Patriarchs, who is the supreme ruler in the heavenly ranks, which is the realm of the world that has territory after the human world. The four great gods act as the worlds (protecting the world) in all four directions. They have to keep the peace to protect the saints who have established their morality in both the human and divine worlds. Furthermore, Duowen Tianwang is also known as "Thep Thammaban" or "Hu Huab." he is the Dharma guardian or keeper of Buddhism and also a guardian deity of various religious sites It also helps to protect the country that values

Buddhism. The Buddha has assigned you the main duty of "Tor Ung Thien Oung" (Maha God who holds the magical umbrella) to help take care of the wind and rain according to the season. So that people can live comfortably It is similar to a great god who assists people in living a prosperous and abundant life. To live well without poverty or suffering, but for humans to be bestowed with wealth and assistance. That must be a good person who follows the morals of the Dharma.

Those born in the year of the Goat should also wear an auspicious pendant. "Thao Chatulokban holds a wonderful umbrella," which you can wear around your neck or carry with you when traveling both near and far. To fill your destiny with auspicious wealth and prosperity in both business and trade. A happy family all year results in greater efficiency and productivity, faster than ever before.

Good Direction: Northwest, Southwest, and East
Bad Direction: Northeast

Lucky Colors: Cream, Gold, Yellow, and Brown.
Lucky Times: 11.00 – 12.59, 13.00 – 14.59, 21.00 – 22.59.
Bad Times: 01.00 – 02.59, 19.00 – 20.59., 23.00 – 00.59

Good Luck For 2023